Hello kids,

I'm your favorite canine pal, Ronny the Frenchie. I'm always up for adventures, and I am here to be your dependable companion on this quest to conquer your world.

Now, when you look at me, you might notice I'm a tad plump, with an irresistibly round and adorable face. Oh, sometimes you may see my cute, wrinkled forehead. That's my thinking spot when faced with a difficult task. And my curly tail? Well, that's my wagging wand of excitement!

I love gazing up at you with my puppy eyes, eagerly absorbing all that you have to say. If you scratch behind my ears, I get lost in a dreamy world of my own. But here's the thing, just like you, from time to time I face challenges with my brain's superpowers. These are also called executive functioning skills. Sometimes, I get distracted, leave tasks half-done, or forget things. But not to worry, I am here to show you some tips and tricks, and together we'll do great!

People have many different words for executive functioning. I like to call it "the CEO of the brain."

It's like the mission control center where you can choose what to do and when, how to act in a certain situation, or plan your schedule.

Executive functioning also helps us put our ideas into action and get things done. Some people think of it as a self-checking system that keeps us on track, making sure we show up for important things like school or birthday parties, do our homework, meet deadlines, and stay organized. The techniques and strategies in this book will help both you and I develop executive functioning skills.

I know we'll make a great team! So, are you ready to join me on this exciting journey?

Let's go!

1

Table of Contents

Ricca's Garden

ricca_garden

info@riccagarden.com

Published & Designed in
Brisbane, Australia
First print: Jan 2024

FREE BONUS

Thanks for coming along with me on thisvv journey to explore all about executive functioning.

Throughout this book, you will discover checklists and charts that you can fill out right in the workbook. Alternatively, you can also print out extra copies using the QR code below.

As an extra bonus, I've included another book featuring the remarkable stories of extraordinary sport heroes and fearless entrepreneurs. I can't wait to share their tales of innovation and determination with you. Plus, there are also some fantastic coloring pages to ignite your creativity!

So, what are you waiting for? Claim these free bonuses by scanning the QR code or type riccagarden.com/ronny_freebies into your web browser.

Your Frenchie,
RONNY

Note to Parents, Caregivers, and Guardians

Dear Parents, Caregivers, and Guardians

We are thrilled to take you on this journey alongside Ronny the Frenchie to help your child with their executive functioning. Chances are you have an awesome and amazing child who is struggling with skills such as organization, planning, and managing their emotions or impulsiveness. Executive functioning encompasses these abilities and more. Read more about the specific areas and skills we'll focus on in the next section.

Remember that not all children will have the same challenges, so it is important to identify any areas in which your child may be struggling and provide them with the necessary support.

In this book, we will explore ways to help build these critical skills with Ronny!

This book is meant to be experienced together with your child. I recommend you read along and work through the activities with them.

Here are some tips for you that will help your child on this journey of self-development:

- Validate your child's feelings. This will help them feel acknowledged and understood.
- Manage your expectations and understand that all children will develop skills at their own pace.
- Engage in self-care. It's important to take care of yourself so you can then, in turn, take care of your children.
- Get professional help if you're struggling or if your child has additional needs.

With the right guidance and support from you, I know your child can be the CEO of their brain. So, with an overjoyed "woof" from Ronny, let's dive right in.

Warm Regards,

Bibi

What is Executive Functioning?

Have you ever struggled with finishing your homework? Or staying focused while in school? How about planning ahead or controlling your big feelings?

I get it! I struggle with those things too.

Now, I've always been a curious and excited pup, ready to explore the world around me, but my executive functioning challenges often get in the way of my adventures. I start exploring something new and exciting, but soon get distracted by something else and forget what I was initially doing. Like the time I was chasing after a butterfly in the park, only to be sidetracked by a squirrel running up a tree. Before I knew it, I had completely forgotten about the butterfly and was now focused on the squirrel.

Or like the time I was happily playing with a cardboard box when I remembered I had an essay to write for school. As I sat down to write it, I needed help getting started. Once I broke down my task into smaller parts, it was way easier to do!

Remember how I said executive functioning is like the CEO or the boss of your brain.

It's what helps you plan ahead, prioritize tasks, stay focused, and control your emotions. Think of it as a little voice inside your head that tells you what to do and when to do it. It helps you remember your homework, stay on track during class, and plan ahead for special events.

Here are the essential skills, aka brain superpowers, that make up executive functioning. We'll conquer them together:

Starting tasks
This is when you're able to quickly begin something important, such as homework or chores, even if you're playing or doing something fun. It's the ability to switch from playtime to essential activities without waiting or putting it off.

Finishing tasks
This means completing what you have started, like finishing your homework, cleaning your room, or playing a game until the end.

Controlling your impulses
Exercising restraint by stopping and thinking before you do something, like resisting the temptation of grabbing the last cookie even though it looks delicious or refraining from blurting something out before you think about it first.

Focusing
Focusing is paying attention and not getting distracted. It's like listening to your teacher without daydreaming or being able to hold your attention on something you need to finish.

Time management
Time management is making a plan for your day, so you have enough time for play, homework, and everything else you want to do.

Memory

Memory is remembering things. It's like remembering where you put your toys or what you learned in school.

Flexibility

This means being able to go with the flow and try new things, like playing a different game if your friends want to or having to change plans at the last minute.

Understanding and managing your emotions

Understanding your emotions is knowing how you feel, like being happy or sad. Managing them is making sure you don't linger in a negative emotional state for too long.

Planning and goal setting

Planning is making a list or a map for what you want to do. Goal setting is deciding what you want to achieve, like learning to tie your shoes or how many books you want to read this month.

Organization

Keeping your things tidy and in order, like putting toys in one place and clothes in another. It helps you find stuff easily.

Woah! It may seem daunting but, with my help, we can tackle it all. Everyone is learning these skills in school, at home and in the world, but sometimes our executive functioning skills need a bit of a boost. And that's exactly what we're going to do.

Ready? Set? Boost!

Getting to Know Yourself

Hey Pals, before we get started on our journey, let's get to know the very special and amazing person you are.

Getting to know yourself is important because it helps you understand your strengths and weaknesses, how to best approach challenges and tasks, and be the best version of you! So, let's take some time to reflect on some things about yourself that make you unique and wonderful.

I'll go first!

I've always been a bit of an explorer at heart, eager to make friends with new dogs and discover new places. But here's the twist – I spotted a pattern in my behavior. You see, I'd start tasks with all the excitement in the world, but sticking with them to the end? Well, that was the tricky part. This realization was a game-changer for me.

As I mulled over my challenges, I zoomed in on a couple of things: focus and time management. I realized my curiosity and boundless enthusiasm sometimes led me on detours to exciting new places, making it tough to finish what I started. Meeting goals and staying on track were real headscratchers.

With this realization, I got to work. I started by setting small, achievable goals for myself. For example, I challenged myself to complete a puzzle or practice my frisbee-catching for a solid 10 minutes without getting sidetracked. To enhance my time-management skill, I started using a planner and a timer to organize my days effectively.

Now, it's your turn, kids!

The upcoming activities will help you discover more about yourself.

Activity 1
All About You

First, think about your favorite hobbies or activities. What do you enjoy doing in your free time? Maybe you love playing sports, dancing, drawing, or reading. Whatever it is, think about why you enjoy it. Is it because it helps you relax, or because it challenges you in a fun way?

My favorite activity:

I enjoy _____ because _____

Now, think about some things that are challenging for you.

Maybe it's starting a new project, remembering to turn in homework, or controlling your emotions when you're upset. It's okay to have things that are difficult for you – we all do! – but it's important to recognize them so we can work on improving them.

I find it challenging to _____

Lastly, think about some things that make you unique and special.

Maybe you have a great sense of humor, or you're really good at comforting your friends when they're sad.

I am good at _____

How did you do, kids? Is it a bit tricky to write about what you're awesome at and what might be challenging? Not to worry! Whether it feels easy or a bit tough, in the next activities there are questions to help you learn even more about yourself. Let's go!

Activity 2
Self-Exploration

Let's start with some questions to help you understand where you feel powerful and where you need support. Circle never, sometimes, often, or always for the following statements:

Aim:
Being self-aware and honest with yourself about your strengths and weaknesses.

1. It's hard for me to finish homework or other tasks.

       Never   Sometimes   Often   Always

2. My room is pretty messy.

       Never   Sometimes   Often   Always

3. It's hard to pay attention in class.

       Never   Sometimes   Often   Always

4. Sitting still in class can be a challenge.

       Never   Sometimes   Often   Always

5. Getting ready for school in the morning is tough.

       Never   Sometimes   Often   Always

6. There are projects that I've left half-finished.

       Never   Sometimes   Often   Always

7. I'm always losing things.

       Never   Sometimes   Often   Always

8. I get in trouble when I don't mean to, like when I get excited.

       Never   Sometimes   Often   Always

9. I give up easily when something gets too boring or frustrating.

       Never   Sometimes   Often   Always

10. It's hard to manage my big feelings like when I'm angry.

       Never   Sometimes   Often   Always

11. I get in trouble at school for things like getting out of my chair or talking.

       Never   Sometimes   Often   Always

12. I don't notice when I am hungry or tired until someone tells me.

       Never   Sometimes   Often   Always

13. When I have a big project at school, I don't know how to get started or what to

do first.

       Never   Sometimes   Often   Always

> Is there another challenge you're facing? Jot it down here.

Activity 3
Reflection

I sat at my desk, looking at the completed questionnaire I had just filled out. As I read through my answers, I felt a sense of dismay settling over me. It was like a spotlight had been shone on my weaknesses and shortcomings, and I couldn't hide from them any longer.

I thought about the times I had given up on a task because it was too hard or too boring. I thought about the mess in my room and the way I always lost things. I thought about the times when I had been in trouble for talking in class or not paying attention.

The more I thought about it, the worse I felt. But wait, I began to experience a different feeling.

It was a feeling of determination.

I realized that I didn't have to be defined by my weaknesses. I could work on them and improve.

I thought back to the goals I had set for myself, the small ones like completing a puzzle or practicing frisbee-catching for 10 minutes without getting distracted. I realized that these goals were the first steps toward building discipline and self-control. I decided to take action and set up a schedule for myself, allocating specific times for homework, cleaning my room, and other tasks.

As I reflected further on my answers, I realized that there were also areas where I felt strong and capable.

I had a vivid imagination and loved drawing and storytelling. I was good at making friends and was always the first to help someone in need.

I felt a sense of pride as I listed these strengths down.

realized that focusing on my strengths could also help me build my self-confidence and resilience.

s I finished my reflection, I felt a sense of clarity and purpose. I knew that there would be challenges ahead, ut I was ready to face them and grow from them.

What are your thoughts and feelings about the struggles you wrote about in Activity 2? Do you feel determined, worried, excited, or enthusiastic?

What do you find hardest?

What do you find easiest?

What are your strengths?

Activity 4
Visualizing Success

After all the deep self-reflection in our previous activities, let's now explore how you would feel if you successfully overcame all your struggles. Close your eyes for a few minutes and picture yourself acing all the challenges that come your way. Can you think of the positive impact that this will have on your daily life?

Below is your canvas for visualizing the empowered and successful you. Draw or write about what this incredible version of yourself would be like. You can also cut and paste images or words from magazines or other printed materials to create a collage.

In the Morning

Mornings are super-duper important as they set the stage for the whole day and lay the groundwork for what's to come later. This section will help us establish a good morning routine that will get us off on the right foot or in my case, paw!

You know what I've realized? Mornings are my favorite time of day. I wake up feeling refreshed and think about all the glorious things that await me.

Let me tell you a bit about my morning routine:

1. I kickstart my day by taking a few deep breaths and stretching my body. Ah, stretches feel so good! This helps me feel calm and energized.

2. Next, I make my bed and tidy my room. I know that having a clean and organized space will help me get off to a good start.

3. Then comes my favorite part of the morning, breakfast! Fueling my body is so important for my brain to function at its best. My go-to breakfast is a bowl of kibble with a side of oatmeal. Yum!

4. After that, I pull out my planner and review any tasks or activities I have lined up for the day. This way, I can mentally prepare myself for what's ahead of me and make sure that I have everything I need.

5. Finally, before heading off into the world, I give myself a little pep talk – a few words of encouragement – and let myself know that anything is possible with hard work and dedication. That always puts me in a great headspace before starting my day!

Now it's your turn! Join me for the next activity to create your paw-some morning routine!

Activity 5
My Morning Routine

Aim:
Establish a morning routine and create a positive mindset to start the day off right!

Let's fill in the checklist below with all the steps you typically do in the morning. Alternatively, you can print out a new copy of the checklist by scanning the QR code on page 4. Feel free to get it laminated and hang it up in your room, so you can see it every morning and stay organized!

Some typical steps include:

Stretch

Make bed

Brush teeth

Get dressed

Eat breakfast

Wear shoes

Grab bag

My Morning Routine

☐ -

☐ -

☐ -

☐ -

☐ -

☐ -

Activity 6
The Time-Guessing Game

Aim:
Be able to guess how
long each task takes
to complete.

For this activity you will need a timer or a stopwatch.

You know kids, I was not always the punctual and organized bulldog that I am today. I was always late for everything. I would oversleep, take forever to get dressed, and then get distracted by my toys or TV. My mom would always tell me to manage my time better, but I didn't really understand what that meant. So, she came up with this awesome game.

It's called "The Time-Guessing Game". Mom would give me a task to complete, like brushing my teeth or making my bed, and I had to guess how long it would take me. We would set a timer, and then the fun began! We would see who was closer to the actual time it took.

You want to know the result?

Well, in the first round, it was all about making my bed. I guessed it would take me 2 minutes but, whoops, it actually took me 5 minutes. Mom was the winner of that round. Next, it was about brushing my teeth. I guessed 1 minute, but it took me 2 minutes. Mom won again!

We played a few more rounds. Guess what? I started to get better at guessing how long tasks would take me. But more importantly, I started to understand the importance of time management. By knowing how long tasks took, I could better plan my day and make sure I was on time for everything.

So, if you're struggling with time management, why not give "The Time-Guessing Game" a try? It's a super fun way to learn how long tasks take and sharpen your time management skills.

Now, here's how to play:

1. In the time-guessing table, list out the tasks you do for your morning routine again.

2. Before you start a task, try to guess how long it will take you to complete it. Write down your guess.

3. Start the task, and time yourself using a stopwatch or timer. Make sure to focus on the task and avoid distractions.

4. Once you've completed the task, stop the timer and write down the actual time it took.

5. Compare your guess to the actual time and see how close you were. If you were spot on, high-five! If not, no problem – just think about why you might have underestimated or overestimated the time.

6. Keep the game going with different tasks. You will soon become more aware of how long a task takes and become a time-guessing pro.

Time-Guessing Table

Task	How long I think it will take	How long it took

Activity 7
Affirmations

I usually hop out of bed each morning full of excitement
but today my day seems a bit daunting. I have a big test in history class and I'm worried I won't do well. But then, as I get ready, I remember something extraordinary – the affirmations I wrote down on a sticky note last night!

You see, our brains are like sponges, and they soak up everything we say. By telling ourselves positive things, we can change our outlook in the morning to a positive one.

Here are the affirmations I wrote down for the upcoming test:

- I am capable and prepared for this test.
- I have studied and know the material well.
- I will do my best and that is enough.

I repeated these affirmations to myself throughout the day, and guess what happened? I felt more and more confident as the hours passed. When I walked into history class, I felt a sense of calm wash over me and began to tackle the test with a clear mind.

Later that day, when I received my test back, I was pleased to see that I had done well.

Now it's your turn!

Cut out 3 affirmations that you want to use and stick them onto your mirror so you can say them to yourself every morning. You can cut out more as you go along.

If you want to keep your workbook in good shape, remember you can always download the affirmations using the QR code on page 4.

I am **capable** of achieving my goals.

Mistakes help me **learn** and **grow**.

I am **unique** and **special** in my own way.

I am *in charge* of my thoughts and emotions.

I believe in myself and my **abilities**.

Challenges make me **stronger**

I have the **POWER** to make a difference in the **WORLD**.

Activity 8
Name it to Tame it

You know, we all have one of those days when things just don't seem to go our way. I've had my fair share of them. Have you? Yesterday, I woke up feeling grumpy and everything just seemed to be going wrong. I spilled breakfast on my shirt, couldn't find my favorite toy, and then got into an argument with my little sister, Daisy. I felt frustrated, angry, and sad all at once and it was hard to manage my emotions.

But you know what? That's when my mom stepped in and taught me about labeling my feelings. She explained that we can better understand and manage our emotions when we can name them. So, we sat down together and talked about how I was feeling, using words like frustrated, angry, and sad.

As we talked, I started to feel a little better. I realized it was perfectly okay to feel these emotions and that I didn't have to hide them or pretend like everything was okay. I also learned some strategies for managing my emotions, like taking deep breaths or going for a walk to calm down when I'm all fired up or feeling down.

Now, whenever I'm having a bad day, I try to label my emotions. And you can do it too!

Name it to tame it!

Naming our emotions is a powerful way to help us stay calm and in control. Do you know the meaning of the emotions below? On the next page, draw faces to match them.

Happy
Angry
Frustrated
Annoyed

Disappointed
Jealous
Sad
Worried

Happy

Disappointed

Angry

Jealous

Frustrated

Sad

Annoyed

Worried

When did you feel them?

How do you cope with your big feelings?

School is a fun and exciting part of the day.

We not only get to see our friends and play, but we also get to learn all sorts of cool stuff. After I finish my morning routine, I'm ready to head off to school with my tail wagging!

You see, I'm always a curious bulldog with loads of interesting questions in my head. Like for example: "Why do some dogs bark louder than others?" and "Why does the sky turn orange at sunset?"

While I love learning new things and playing with my friends during recess, I also know that school requires me to put my executive functioning skills into action. Sometimes this is overwhelming for me when I have to wait my turn, focus on the teacher, and manage my feelings. But I'm up for the challenge!

I know that if I want to succeed in school, I must put my brainpower to work and be the true CEO of my brain when I'm there.

Activity 9
S.T.O.P.

Aim:
Learn how to pause and think before speaking.

I was in Mr. Johnson's class, and he is my favorite teacher of all-time. Why? Because he taught the class about the incredible solar system, and I was so fascinated.

As I sat there and marveled at the images of the planets and stars on the whiteboard. I felt like I could almost touch the craters of the moon! I wondered what it would be like to explore them. The vastness of space and its endless possibilities filled my thoughts but, oops, my excitement got the better of me.

Mr. Johnson asked the class a question and Max, my friend, began to answer. Without giving it a second thought, I blurted out the answer, cutting Max off mid-sentence. Sometimes it was hard for me to wait my turn to speak.

But here's the cool part:

Mr. Johnson, being the awesome teacher he was, turned this into a valuable lesson. He explained that sometimes we may feel the need to say something right away, but it's important to take a moment to pause and think before responding.

He asked all of us to practice taking a deep breath and counting to 3 before responding to a question or comment. It was like a secret code to ensure we'd thought about our words first.

Now you try it! You can use the word STOP to help you remember:

Stop talking and moving. Take a deep breath!

Think about what you want to say

Observe the environment around you. What is happening?

Proceed

Activity 10
Checking and Rechecking Your Work

Tip to parents:
Instead of doing your child's work or checking it for them, try guiding them through the process. This way your child can learn how to develop the skills to self-assess and become more self-reliant.

Aim:
Check your work before turning it in.

Let me take you back to a beautiful autumn day. The sky was a brilliant blue and the leaves painted the trees in shades of golden yellows and fiery reds. The ground was a cozy carpet of crunchy leaves. Fall, with its fresh scent in the air, was just paw-some. I couldn't wait to go out for recess, but I had to finish my math worksheet first.

I was doing really well and feeling proud of myself for completing it so fast. But when I turned it in, my teacher, Ms. Percy, pointed out some careless mistakes I had made.

Oops! Don't worry, she shared some cool tricks to help me reduce those oopsie moments.

She taught me some strategies, like double-checking my work and reviewing the instructions before starting the assignment.

I also learned the importance of taking my time and not rushing through my work. When I slowed down and focused on each problem, I found that I made fewer mistakes. Now, when I'm working on an assignment, I go through a series of steps to make sure I do my very best.

Here's what I learned:

1. Read the instructions carefully. I make sure I understand the instructions before I start working on the assignment. This helps me avoid mistakes and saves me time in the long run.

2. Read the problem out loud. This helps me to understand what's going on and spot any sneaky mistakes that might be hiding.

3. Draw a picture of the problem. I like to doodle a bit. Sometimes, drawing a picture of the problem helps me understand it better and figure out how to solve it.

4. Circle the keywords. Be a detective on a mission! Circle the important words in the problem to make it easier to pick the right operation and solve the problem.

5. Set up the problem. I make sure I set up the problem correctly before I start solving it. You can ask the teacher for help if you need to for this step.

6. Do the problem. I solve the problem step by step, making sure I don't skip any steps or make any careless mistakes.

7. Check my work. Once I've solved the problem, I double-check my work to make sure it's correct.

You can use these very same steps when you have a problem or assignment.

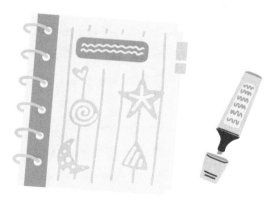

Activity 11
Focus and Mindfulness

Aim:
Learn how to stay focused by practicing mindfulness.

Ughh!! I'm sitting in class trying to focus on what the teacher is saying but I keep getting distracted by the birds chirping outside. Birdsong echoes through the room melodically. The notes of one of them spark a memory from long ago, when my mother would sing me to sleep. Oh no, I am getting distracted again.

I try to shake my head to clear my thoughts and refocus on the lesson. Learning requires focus after all. Yet sometimes it's hard to focus, especially when there are so many distractions.

Now, imagine focus as your superpower flashlight in a dark room.

It helps you shine your light on your most important task while keeping all the other distractions away. Your focus helps you navigate through your tasks and helps you stay on course when you need to work for a long period of time. It's your attention span in action!

So, here's why it's important to do some self-monitoring. You can check in with yourself from time to time and ask,

"Am I paying attention?"

If the answer is no, steer your wheel back on course. One way to do this is by practicing mindfulness.

Mindfulness is like paying attention to the present moment without judgment. We can take a deep breath and focus on our breathing as we breathe in and breathe out. This helps us clear our minds and refocus on the task.

Ultimately, focusing takes practice and effort. But with the right strategies and mindset, we can improve.

So, here's a fun exercise to try:

Sit in a quiet place and focus on your breathing for 2 minutes. You can use a small hourglass timer to help.

Pay attention to your breathing. In and out. As you breathe, focus on breathing in and breathing out. Focus on just one thing at a time. When your thoughts drift away like leaves down a stream, gently bring them back to your breathing.

Afterwards, reflect on how it feels to focus and how it differs from when your mind wanders. Next time, increase your time to 4 minutes and you'll find that focusing gets a lot easier with practice.

You can use this trick to regain your focus again when you need to read or complete an assignment. When you feel distracted or frustrated, focus on your breathing before continuing.

How does it feel to focus?

Activity 12
The Where, When, and Why of Negative Feelings

I'm a pretty happy bulldog. I usually have a bright smile that lights up my face and my whole body is beaming with joy. But even happy bulldogs, like me, have days when they feel sad or angry. Our emotions are like a rainbow, with many different colors, including some that aren't so bright.

One day, I was playing with my friends during recess when I accidentally tripped and fell.

My friends didn't mean any harm, but they couldn't help giggling. That made me feel embarrassed and angry. I had an urge to lash out and yell at them, but I remembered the handy tools I'd learned in class.

I took a deep breath and asked myself: "Where is the emotion coming from? When did it start? Why am I feeling this way?" I realized that I was feeling embarrassed and angry because I didn't want my friends to see me as clumsy.

I took another deep breath and thought about healthy ways to respond to my emotions.

Instead of bottling it up, I decided to approach my friends and tell them how I felt. I said, "When you laughed at me, it hurt my feelings. I know it was an accident, but it's not nice to make fun of someone when they fall."

And guess what? My friends apologized, and I felt better knowing that I spoke up for myself and managed to handle the situation in a healthy way. Sometimes, all it takes is a conversation.

Now let's explore situations when you've had to manage your emotions. Remember that all emotions are okay to feel, even the not-so-bright ones. The key is to understand our triggers and how to manage those big feelings. Fill in the table below:

Emotion	When	Where	Why (Your Trigger)	Healthy Ways to Respond
Angry				
Sad				
Frustrated				
Embarrassed				
Excited				

Here are some more ideas to respond to big feelings !

- Count to 10 before you take an action, to prevent an impulsive reaction.
- Take a Deep Breath to help you feel calm.
- Ask a grown-up for help.
- Talk it out and share your feelings with someone you trust.
- Walk away and take a break to calm down.

Activity 13
Considering Other People's Feelings

Aim:
Understand how our emotions can impact others and why it's important to consider other people's feelings.

I was walking home from school when I saw my friend Max sitting alone on a bench. Max looked sad and upset, and I could tell that something was bothering him. Naturally, I stopped and asked if he was okay.

Max opened up to me and shared that he was having a tough time at home. He felt like everything was piling up and he didn't know how to handle the situation. As he spoke, I could see the pain in his eyes and hear the sadness in his voice.

That's when I realized my friend needed someone to listen to him and be there for him.

So, I sat with Max and just listened to what he had to say. I didn't try to solve his problems or give him advice, but I just listened with empathy and understanding.

36

I was there, fully present for him, offering words of support and encouragement. I made sure he knew I'd be there whenever he needed someone to talk to.

That's what empathy is all about - being there for others in their time of need.

Empathy helps us build strong and meaningful relationships with others and it is something that we should all practice.

As we talked, I could see a change in Max. He started to relax, and a little smile even appeared. It might not have been a huge change, but I knew I had made a difference just by being there for him.

From that day on, I made a promise to check in on Max and other friends when they were feeling down or upset. I learned that sometimes, all it takes is a listening ear and a kind heart to make someone feel better. Now, it's your turn to practice some empathy.

Think of a time when someone showed you kindness or understanding when you were feeling upset or down. How did it make you feel? How did it impact your day?

Now, think of ways that you can show empathy toward others. It can be as simple as offering a kind word or gesture, or just being there to listen when someone needs to talk.

Activity 14
Being Kind

It was "Thoughtful Thursday" at school, and we had a fantastic time in class discussing the topic of the day – how small acts of kindness can have a big impact on others.

We all shared stories and examples of kindness and how we could sprinkle kindness everywhere we go.

My teacher gave us a challenge: perform one act of kindness every day for a week. I was all in, thinking about all the different ways I could be kind to others.

I held the door open for someone who had their hands full, gave a big thumbs-up to a classmate's artwork, and even shared my snacks with a friend who forgot theirs. Every small act felt like planting a seed of happiness.

By the end of the week, I felt super proud of all the kind things I had done for others.

But here's the cool part - I noticed that my acts of kindness were having a ripple effect!

Others were inspired to be kind too. And it made my heart feel all warm and fuzzy.

Being kind is like a magic wand you carry in your heart. It's a simple but powerful way to spread positivity and make the world a better place.

It's important to keep in mind that when we are being kind, we do so without wanting or asking for anything in return. So, for example, when I help my friends or share my toys, I do so because I care for them, not because I want them to also share their toys or do something for me. Think about some ways you can be kind.

Write them on the leaves of the Kindness Tree.

Activity 15
Growth Mindset & the Power of Positive Thinking

Aim:
Develop a growth mindset and learn how to reframe negative thoughts into positive ones.

Hey kids, have you ever felt frustrated? Well, I have. When I'm frustrated, my tail doesn't wag very much, my ears droop down and my brows start to crease. Let me share one of those moments with you.

I was in math class learning about fractions. But no matter how hard I tried, I just couldn't seem to get it right. I kept making mistakes and I started to feel like a failure. I thought to myself, "I'll never be good at math. I'm just not smart enough." But then, a light bulb moment happened. I recalled something I'd learned about having a growth mindset.

A growth mindset is like a beacon of light in the darkness, radiating positivity and optimism.

It's all about believing that abilities are like muscles; they can be worked out, trained, and grown. A growth mindset is all about knowing you can build those "muscles." Whereas a "fixed mindset" makes you believe that your abilities are set in stone and you either have it or you don't.

With my newfound growth mindset, I told myself something different. I took a deep breath and reframed my negative thought into a positive one. If I worked hard, I could achieve anything by learning from my mistakes and never giving up. I said to myself, "I may not understand this problem right now, but I can learn and improve with practice."

Positive self-talk and a growth mindset are my secret weapons to help me overcome challenges and reach my goals. Here are some affirmations that I use, and you can too:

- I am capable of learning and growing.
- I can do hard things.
- Mistakes help me learn and improve.
- I am not good at this – YET!

What are some positive things you can say to yourself to help you get through your day?

Here's your exciting mission! Pick a goal or challenge that you want to achieve. Write down any negative thoughts that pop into your head about that goal, and then reframe them into positive affirmations using a growth mindset. Use the table below:

Goal:	
Your negative thoughts	Your positive thoughts & affirmations

Activity 16
Action Plans

I had a big project all about recycling and taking care of the planet. Now, I really do love recycling, but this project felt like a mountain of tasks towering over me. I felt overwhelmed and stressed out as the project seemed too big to tackle all at once.

That's when my teacher said she would teach us how to make an action plan.

So, I took out my trusty notebook and wrote "My school project on recycling" and started breaking down the project into smaller, manageable steps. My teacher helped me with this:

1. First, we listed all the tasks that needed to be completed, like brainstorming, research, writing, and putting it all together.
2. Then, I prioritized them based on their importance and deadline. Consider doing the most important or harder tasks first.
3. Finally, I set a timeline for when I would complete each task.

With my action plan in place, I felt more confident and in control of the project. And you know what? I was able to complete each task on time, and even finished the project ahead of schedule.

Creating an action plan is a great way to tackle big tasks and goals. Here are some steps to help you create your own action plan:

1. Write down the task or goal you want to achieve. Break it down into smaller, manageable steps.
2. Prioritize the steps based on their importance and deadline.
3. Decide when you need to complete each task.

With your action plan in place, you'll conquer tasks like a champ! Remember to estimate how long each step will take, and don't forget to reward yourself each step of the way.

Is there a task that you need to complete soon? Try and create an action plan below:

Task / Goal:

Due date:

Steps: Deadline:

1.   /   /

2.   /   /

3.   /   /

4.   /   /

5.   /   /

6.   /   /

Activity 17
The Buddy System

I've got a story to share with you about how I used the buddy system to get things done.

You see, there was this one time when I had a big project all about the history of bones (you know, because I'm a dog, and bones are kind of my thing). At first, I was really excited to dive into the project but, as time went on, I found myself slacking off and getting easily distracted.

That's when I remembered what my wise teacher had told me about the buddy system!

The idea was to work in pairs so we could keep each other on track and motivated. So, I asked my best friend and classmate, Fluffy the poodle, to be my trusty accountability buddy.

We made a plan to work on our projects together every evening. Fluffy would come over to my house, and we would set up our workspaces side-by-side. Sure, we would take breaks to play fetch and have snacks, but we would always get right back to work.

And you know what? Having Fluffy there made all the difference. I felt more motivated to work on my project because I didn't want to let her down. And she was always there to give me support and help when I got stuck.

In the end, we both finished our projects on time and got great grades! And it was all thanks to the buddy system.

So, if you're having trouble staying motivated or need some extra support, consider teaming up with a friend or family member as an accountability buddy.

Make a plan to work together and encourage each other to stay on track. You might be surprised at how much of a difference it can make!

1. Who could your accountability buddy be? Think of three fantastic people who could do this.

   a. _____

   b. _____

   c. _____

2. Why do you think having an accountability buddy is super important?

   _____

3. What kind of amazing support do you think you could provide your accountability buddy?

   _____

4. How would you plan to work together with your accountability buddy?

   _____

5. Why is the buddy system helpful for achieving goals?

   _____

At Home/ After School

You know the saying, "Home is where the heart is"? Well, I totally understand why. I love everything about being home. Home is a place of warmth and comfort, with soft carpets, cozy furniture, and the inviting smell of home cooking: mashed potatoes and banana bread being my favorite. And let's not forget the laughter and memories that fill every corner, making it a safe space where I can truly be myself.

Activity 18
Creating an After-School Schedule

After a busy day at school, I'm always excited to go back home. I'm greeted with a big smile from Mom, and we usually chat about my day, and I share some of my highlights with her. Then, it's off for a snack and some relaxation on my favorite cushion. What's your favorite after-school snack? Mine would be peanut butter and biscuits with a glass of milk. Yum! As I munch on my snack, I gaze out the window and marvel at the beautiful clouds in the sky.

Now, I have not forgotten my homework and chores. I've got it all figured out! I make sure I get things done with my very own after-school schedule. Want to know what it looks like?

Ronny's After-School Schedule

3pm Snack and relax

4pm Finish my homework

5pm Read my book or go for a walk outdoors

6pm Help Mom with dinner

7pm Dinner. Yum!

8pm Get ready for bed

So, as you can see, after finishing my snack, I start doing my homework. I like to tackle the harder tasks first so that I can feel a sense of accomplishment and motivation to continue. But if you want to start with an easy task, that's absolutely OK!

Once math is checked off, I move on to my history assignment, which is usually a little easier and more enjoyable.

After all that brainwork, I give myself a break to read my favorite book. I love getting lost in a good story, and it helps me to destress and unwind after a long day. Sometimes, instead of reading, I prefer to go for a walk and smell the fresh air. Oh, and flowers too!

Finally, it's dinner time and I get to spend quality moments with my family. We like to talk about our day, share funny stories and, of course, enjoy a delicious meal together. Having an after-school schedule not only helps me stay on track, but also ensures I have time for the things I enjoy.

Now it's your turn to create your own schedule.

Remember that your schedule may be different on different days of the week depending on what after-school activities you have.

Time	Monday	Tuesday	Wednesday	Thursday	Friday
3pm					
4pm					
5pm					
6pm					
7pm					
8pm					
9pm					

Activity 19
Creating a Space That Helps You Focus

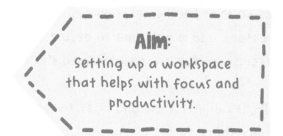

Aim: Setting up a workspace that helps with focus and productivity.

You know, sometimes in life we face challenges that need solving. I've got to say, I have been having trouble focusing lately. Whether it's tackling my homework or just playing with my toys, I find myself getting easily distracted. Luckily, my parents helped me realize I needed a designated space to help me concentrate better. Having a clean and organized space helps my brain super-charge my concentration.

So, I decided to transform my room by clearing out any unnecessary clutter to get rid of distractions. I moved my toys to a separate area and cleared my desk of any non-school-related items.

My desk became my command center.

I organized everything from stationery to textbooks into neat compartments and put them in easy-to-reach

I also snagged a comfy chair that helped me sit for longer periods of time without getting tired.

But hey, it's not just about functionality. I like adding some personal touches to my space too.

I put up some motivational posters to keep me inspired, and I added a small potted plant to my desk to bring a touch of nature indoors. I hung up pictures of my family and friends and put up a bulletin board where I could pin up my favorite quotes or doodles. Having those things around me made me feel more comfortable and at home in my space.

After all my hard work, I couldn't be happier with how everything turned out. I had created a functional and beautiful space, and I was excited to start using it. Whenever I need to focus on my work, I will retreat to my new and improved space and get things done. It is a great feeling to have a designated area that is conducive to productivity and creativity.

Now it's your turn!

On the next page, draw how you'd like your study space to be. Think about how you can transform it into a place to focus. Maybe it's by adding some plants, organizing your supplies, or whatever other wild ideas you can come up with. Make sure it reflects your unique style and helps you reach your goals.

I organized everything from stationery to textbooks into neat compartments and put them in easy-to-reach spots. I also snagged a comfy chair that helped me sit for longer periods of time without getting tired.

Use your imagination. Draw how you'd like your study space to be.

What items do you need while you study? Examples are water, a timer, school supplies, etc.

Activity 20
Procrastination

Note To Parents: Talk with your children about when they tend to break away from studying to procrastinate – during hard tasks? When they get stuck? When they get bored? Having your children reflect on the triggers for procrastination behavior is the start of developing an intervention that can help.

We all have bad habits, right? Well lately I've developed this bad habit of procrastination. Procrastination is when we put something off until the last minute, even if we know we should do it sooner. It can be a tough habit to break but, with a little self-reflection, we can identify our triggers and develop strategies to overcome them.

You see, I'm the king of procrastinators. I'll find any excuse to avoid doing the things I need to do, like chasing my tail or taking a nap. But the problem is, I always end up regretting it later when I'm in a rush to finish my tasks.

One day, I had a big project due for my history class. I was supposed to create a poster about my favorite historical figure. But instead of working on it, I decided to take a long nap and watch some TV.

Before I knew it, it was almost time to go to bed and I hadn't even started. I began to panic and bark like crazy, hoping someone could magically teach me how to do my project in a snap!

I never wanted that to happen again, so I worked with my mom to figure out why I kept putting things off and what I could do about it.

Now, whenever I catch myself procrastinating, I like to take a step back and reflect on why I'm doing it.

Maybe I'm feeling overwhelmed by the task, or maybe I'm just in the mood for something more entertaining. Sometimes, the task itself seems boring. Once I identify my trigger, I can come up with a plan to overcome it.

Now you try it! Is there a task that you often put off doing?

Task	Why am I avoiding it?	What can I do to overcome this?

It can also be helpful to:

1. Break the task into smaller, more manageable parts. This can make it feel less overwhelming and easier to start. Remember, starting is often the hardest part.

2. Set a specific goal and deadline for yourself. Having a goal and deadline can help you stay motivated and focused.

3. Use a timer to work for short periods of time, like 20–30 minutes, and then reward yourself with a break.

Activity 21
Asking for Help

Aim:
Understand that asking for help is OK! Let's learn how to ask for help when you need it.

It's important to remember that we all need help sometimes.

Asking for help is a sign of strength, not weakness.

Think about a time when you asked for help and how it made you feel. Was it scary at first? Did it end up being helpful in the end?

You know, I've always been quite the independent type. I love doing things on my own like getting dressed, preparing for school, and even doing my homework. But recently, I realized that asking for help is perfectly fine.

The other day, I found myself in a tough spot. I was sitting alone in my room, staring blankly at the pile of homework in front of me. I knew I was in trouble. I had always prided myself on being self-sufficient but, this time, I was in over my head. I knew I needed help but the thought of asking for it made me feel weak.

But then, I remembered what our teacher had said about asking for help. It is not a sign of weakness but a sign of strength. It took a lot of courage for me to admit it but I finally reached out to my best friend, Tom, and asked if he could help me out with my math homework.

To my relief, he agreed without hesitation and came over to my house the next day. As we worked through the problems together, I couldn't help but feel grateful for his support. Not only did he help me understand the material, but he also reminded me that it's okay to ask for help from those we trust.

So, remember, don't be afraid to ask for help when you need it. Here are some tips on how to ask for help effectively:

1. Be specific about what you need help with.
2. Choose someone you know and trust to ask for help.
3. Be respectful of their time and be willing to work together to find a solution.
4. Express gratitude for their help and support.

Now think about this:

Who can I ask for help from? Who are my go-to people?

_____

How do I ask for help at home?

_____

How do I ask for help at school?

_____

Let's practice how we can ask for help.

Remember that it's better to request rather than demand help.

- Would you mind helping me with...............................?
- I'm having trouble with............................. . Could you show me how to do it?
- I'm feeling a bit overwhelmed with............................. . Could you help me?
- I could use some help with............................. Could you help me?

Activity 22
Organizing Schoolwork

Aim: Getting papers, folders, and digital files organized.

Don't you hate it when you can't find something you need in your room? Well, that used to happen to me a lot. Once, I had worked hard on my assignment about polar bears in the Arctic, but I couldn't find it! I turned it in late and that was not fun at all!

So, let's rewind back to last year when I was in 2nd grade. I was a bit of a mess when it came to organizing my schoolwork. Papers were scattered all over my room, folders were overflowing with loose pages, and I had no idea where to find anything. I wanted to do a good job on my assignments, but my disorganized mess got in the way. But here's the cool part – I learned some really cool and handy dandy tricks that I'll share with you. These tricks have transformed me into a super organized 3rd grader.

Here's what I did: I came up with a clever system!

A system that ensures everything has its own special place, so you always know where to get what you need in a jiffy!

With my mom's help, we got started. First, we bought different color folders for each subject – blue for science, red for math, and green for English. Then, we organized the papers by date, putting the most recent papers on top. I put the completed work on the right and the to-do work on the left.

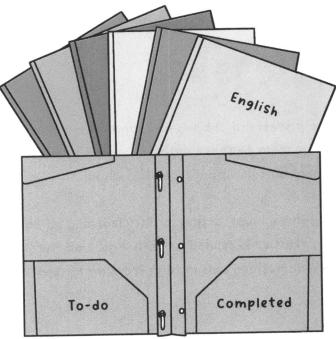

Next, we moved on to my digital files. My mom showed me how to create folders on my computer for each subject. We organized the files by date and assignment name and this makes it easy to find all my digital notes and assignments.

Now it's your turn! Think about how you can organize your own schoolwork and papers.

Here are some tips to get you started:

1. Get folders for each subject and label them with different colors to make them easy to find.
2. Organize your papers by date, with the most recent ones on top.
3. Keep completed work on the right side of the folder and to-do work on the left side.
4. Create folders on your computer for each subject and organize the files by date and assignment name.

Remember, everything has a home. With your fantastic new organization skills, you'll be able to find everything you need in a heartbeat.

Activity 23

Packing Your Backpack Before Bed

Aim: Develop a routine to get your backpack ready at night. This way, mornings are stress-free and you're ready to conquer the day.

I'm a pretty smart pup but sometimes I can forget things. I have a little story to share with you about how I forgot to pack something important in my backpack for school.

So, there I was, sitting in class, learning all about bones (my favorite subject, of course!) But then, my teacher surprised us with a quiz on the skeletal system. I panicked – I knew I had studied for it but something was missing from my backpack.

I searched through my backpack frantically but those bone flashcards I needed? Nowhere to be found!

Then it hit me!

I had forgotten to pack my backpack the night before! I had been so tired after playing fetch with my dad that I just went straight to bed without checking my backpack.

I felt quite silly but luckily my teacher was understanding. She gave me a few extra minutes to study before the quiz and even let me use a spare set of flashcards. Phew!

That day, I learned my lesson - I need to pack my backpack the night before so I don't forget anything important.

Now, I've developed a routine to make sure I'm always prepared for school.

Here's what I do:

First, I designate specific spaces in my backpack for certain items, just like my teacher suggested. I have a front zipper pouch for pencils and supplies, side pockets for water bottles, and the front flap is for my homework folder.

Every night before bed, I go through the list of items I'll need for the next day and pack them in their designated spots in my backpack. This includes my completed homework, textbooks, notes, and anything for special classes like art or PE. Sometimes, I even lay out my clothes for school so I don't have to scramble around in the morning trying to find something to wear.

By sticking to this routine, I haven't forgotten anything important for school again. My mornings are less stressful when everything is perfectly organized.

So kids, developing a routine for packing your backpack before bed is a smart move.

This way you won't forget any essential stuff for school, and you'll be better prepared for the day ahead. Can you show me what your backpack looks like when it's all ready to go?

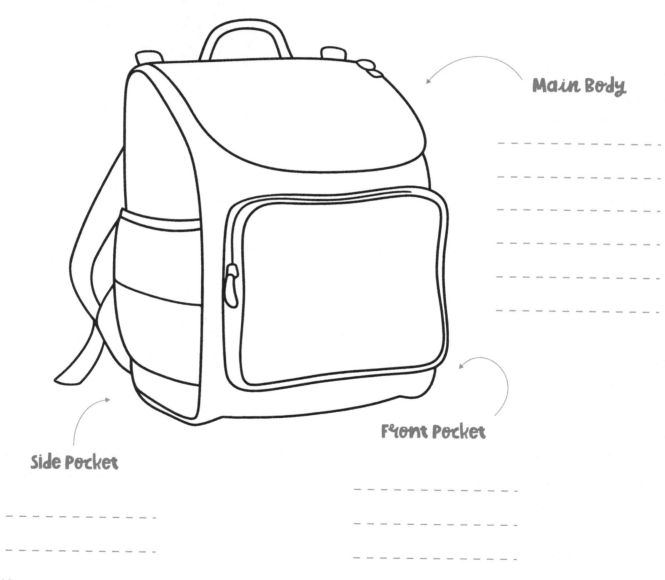

Main Body

- -

- -

- -

- -

- -

- -

Side Pocket

- - - - - - - - - - - - - - - - -

Front Pocket

- - - - - - - - - - - - - - -

- - - - - - - - - - - - - - -

Activity 24
My Super Planner

Now that I'm in 3rd grade, I realize I've got a lot going on in my life. There's homework, after-school activities, hobbies, and fun stuff I plan with family and friends. Keeping track of it all can be a challenge. Here's where a planner comes in handy.

I decided to create my very own "My Super Planner".

It has a monthly view, making it a breeze to jot down all my tasks, goals, and appointments in one place. It's like a snapshot of my whole month so I can plan ahead and make sure I have enough time for important tasks, like studying for a test.

Every Sunday night, I snuggle up with my planner and look at my week ahead. It's like a roadmap, guiding me along the way. With my planner, I can stay organized, focused, and on track with my tasks. I'm definitely a visual person, and I love being able to see what's coming up in the week and month ahead.

Now, let me give you a sneak peek into how it works.

Sunday	Monday	Tuesday	Wednesday	Thursday	Friday	Saturday
					1	2
3	4	5	6 Start studying for Math Exam	7	8	9
10 Buy a Present for Max	11	12	13 Math Exam	14	15	16 Max's Birthday Party
17	18	19	20	21	22	23
24	25	26	27	28 Start Packing for Camping	29	30 Camping
31						

I make sure to write down important dates
and events on my calendar!

So, I've got a math exam coming up and I'm gearing up to study for it a week before. Oh, and my buddy Max's birthday is also around the corner! I've put it on my calendar to plan a trip to the mall with Mom to hunt for the perfect toy. I've also been eagerly waiting for the camping trip at the end of the month. Two days before the trip, I give myself a reminder to start packing up for the wilderness adventure! Can't wait for all the fun!

You see, it's not just about jotting down important dates, I also make plans to get ready a few days before.

It took some trial and error to figure out the best way to organize my planner, but I quickly got the hang of it. I found that having a visual representation of what I needed to do was super helpful. Oh, and guess what? I also added stickers! I love stickers, and it made my planner look so sparkly.

Now let's work on your very own Super Planner.

You can buy a calendar or print out more copies of the monthly planner below by scanning the QR code on page 4.

Month: ## Year:

Sunday	Monday	Tuesday	Wednesday	Thursday	Friday	Saturday

Activity 25
What Can I Do Instead?

I hope you're having a paw-some day because I certainly am. I can say I live a pretty happy life. I'm an upbeat dog and I see my life as a boundless ocean filled with happiness and contentment. I am surrounded by a loving crew of friends and family who've got my back.

But of course, like everyone, I am no exception to those moments of stress that can creep up on all of us.

I noticed that whenever I felt stressed or upset, I would turn to video games as a way to distract myself. But I realized that this wasn't a healthy way to cope with my emotions because video games don't offer any support and I can easily lose track of time playing them, so I wanted to find an alternative.

I talked to my dad about it, and he suggested I try a new hobby or activity that I might enjoy. That's when I discovered my love for drawing!

Now, whenever stress hits, I pull out my sketchbook and start drawing. It's a relaxing and creative way to process my emotions and take my mind off things.

Oh, here's another cool trick I learned:

I've got this awesome stress ball. Whenever I'm feeling a bit impulsive, I give it a good squeeze. It really does the trick!

Recognizing when our habits or behaviors aren't serving us well is important.

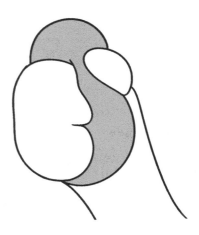

Here are some steps to help you find an alternative path:

1. Identify the habit or behavior you want to change. Some examples may be engaging in too much screen time or not putting away your things where they belong.
2. Reflect on why you engage in the behavior and how it makes you feel.
3. Now, think about alternative behaviors that can give you that same sense of comfort or help you navigate those tricky emotions .

Fill in the table below:

Habit or behavior I want to cahnge	How does it makes me feel?	What can I do instead?

Activity 26
Sibling Rivalry

I love my little sister Daisy but, let's face it, there are times when we can't seem to get along. Daisy, with her bright brown eyes, is always full of energy and enthusiasm. She loves to laugh, and she loves to complete her look with sparkly jewelry.

Despite her small size, she is fearless and demands attention. She can be mischievous at times but she has a heart of gold. Sometimes, it's like we're constantly competing with each other, trying to prove who's better, smarter, or more talented. And trust me, it gets exhausting and it often leads to arguments and hurt feelings.

The other day, I sat on my bed, simmering with frustration.

We'd had yet another heated argument, and Daisy had just stormed out of the room. It seemed like we were always fighting lately, and I was tired of it. I knew I had to find a way to manage my emotions and figure out how to get along with her.

I took a deep breath and decided to go and find Daisy. I found her in her room, sitting on her bed with her arms crossed.

"Hey," I said tentatively.

"What do you want?" she replied harshly.

"I just wanted to say sorry for what I said earlier. I didn't mean it."

Daisy softened a bit and we began talking about what was really bothering us. It turned out that we were both stressed about other stuff that was causing us to lash out at each other.

We made a pact right there, promising to be there for each other and really listen when the other one needed to talk.

From that day forward, our relationship improved drastically. Sure, we still had our moments of rivalry but we were better equipped to handle them. We made an effort to communicate more effectively and to respect each other's boundaries. Plus, we even started doing fun activities together, like playing board games and baking cookies.

Here are some tips that can help next time you have a fight with your sibling:

1. Take a step back and assess the situation before reacting. Ask yourself if this is really a big deal or can it be worked out?
2. Try to communicate calmly and listen to what your sibling has to say.
3. Respect each other and remember that it's OK to disagree.

Can you think of a time when you had a fight with your sibling? What happened?

What can you do differently next time?

Activity 27
Checking In on Your Workspace

Aim:
To check in and see if your workspace is being maintained.

Tip for Parents: Set a day each month to tidy up and check in on your child's workspace. Talk to them about what's working well and what needs to be changed.

Remember how I created my very own workspace in Activity 19? Well, I have to say, it's been going pretty well!

At first, I was a little hesitant about the whole thing. I mean, I've never been much of a neat freak, and having a designated study area seemed like a lot of effort. But my mom helped me set it up, and now I absolutely love it.

I have my very own desk with a lamp and a comfy chair. All my school supplies are organized in drawers and there's a shelf for my favorite books. And best of all, there are no distractions! No more chasing my tail or staring out the window when I should be studying.

Now, when it's time to do my homework, I head straight to my workspace. I like to light my lamp and turn on some calming music – it helps me focus. And when I need a break, I can always take a quick walk around the room or grab a snack from the nearby kitchen.

Even though I love my study area, I still have to check in and make sure it's being maintained.

Once a month, I take some time to tidy up my space and make sure everything is in its place. I start by clearing off my desk and giving it a good wipe with a damp cloth. Then, I go through my drawers and shelves to make sure everything is where it belongs. I like to take this time to also throw away any old papers or supplies that I no longer need.

After I've tidied up, I sit down and think about my workspace. What's working well for me? What needs to be changed or improved? Is there anything missing that would make my study area even better?

It's important to regularly check in on your workspace to make sure it's still doing its job and helping you stay productive. Plus, it's always nice to have a clean and organized space to work in. So, take some time to do your own workspace check-in! You might be surprised at how much it can improve your productivity and overall work experience.

Here's your handy checklist:

1. Clear off your desk and give it a wipe with a damp cloth.

2. Go through your drawers and shelves to make sure everything is organized and in its place.

3. Throw away any old papers or supplies that you no longer need.

4. Reflect on your workspace. What's working well, and what could be improved?

5. Make any necessary adjustments to supercharge your productivity and work experience.

Activity 28
Checking In on Your Schedule

Hi kids! Phew, today I was having a super busy day with loads of things on my plate. I had karate class after school, homework to do and had to help my mom with some yard work. Sometimes, it's hard to keep up with everything when I have a lot to do.

I have a schedule to help me stay on track (remember the one I made in Activity 18?) It's got all sorts of stuff on it, including time for schoolwork, exercise, and play. I also added specific times for meals and bedtime.

At first, I was excited about my new schedule. I felt more organized and productive than ever before. But you know what happened after a few weeks? I started to slip up. I would stay up late watching TV instead of going to bed on time, or I would spend too much time playing and forget all about my homework.

Just like keeping your workspace in order, it's important to regularly check in on your schedule. That way, you can make sure you're sticking to it and making the most of your time.

The same goes for the Super Planner that we created together for Activity 24. Once a week, I like to sit down with my planner and go over my plans for the coming days.

First things first, I make sure all my activities and deadlines are still accurate and up-to-date. Then, I take a look at my to-do list and make sure I'm making progress on each task.

If I notice that I'm falling behind on something, I start to wonder why. Maybe the task is more difficult than I anticipated, or maybe I'm not managing my time effectively. Once I figure out the problem, I make a plan to tackle it.

Sometimes, it's as simple as breaking the task down into smaller, more manageable parts, or I may need to adjust my schedule to allow for more time to complete it.

But you know, checking in on my schedule isn't just about catching up on tasks I've fallen behind on. It's also about making sure I'm taking care of myself and balancing my activities. I make sure I'm getting enough sleep, eating healthy meals, and taking breaks to relax and have fun.

So, take some time to check in on your own schedule. Here are some things to ponder over:

1. Are you making the most of your time?
2. Are you taking care of yourself? If not, make some adjustments.
3. What do you need to change in your schedule so it can work better for you?

Household Chores

Hey kids! Do you have household chores that you have to do?

I do. Actually, both my sister Daisy and I have chores that we do every day. I set the table and clean up after dinner, while Daisy takes charge of loading the dishwasher. Oh, and I get to be the official trash helper with my dad.

Now, when we first started with chores, we did our fair share of grumbling. But then, our parents sat us down and explained something essential: chores aren't just about getting stuff done; they are about learning life skills and becoming a responsible family member.

I get it, though. Doing chores can be hard sometimes. It's hard to get started, let alone finishing them. It may mean switching from something fun to a task that seems less exciting, and we have to keep our focus on the task until it's done. Luckily there are ways to power up these skills. The activities in this section will help you work on the skills needed to get all your chores (and other tasks) done in no time!

Activity 29
Household Chores Chart

Tip for Parents: Talk to your child about your expectations for how well they do their chores. Discuss how putting in the time and effort leads to higher quality results.

I wanted to tell you about how my family started using a household chores chart to keep track of our responsibilities and motivate us to get our chores done. It's sort of like having a Family Control Center to tell us what to do!

Back in the day, my sister Daisy and I would argue about who had to do what chores and when. It was frustrating for everyone involved. But guess what? Our clever parents came up with this brilliant idea of a Household Chores Chart.

On our chart, we have our names across the top and all the chores listed down the side. My job is to set the table and clean up after dinner, while Daisy's is to handle the dishwasher. Even our parents have their own chores, like doing the laundry and cleaning the bathrooms.

Now, here's the fun part – rewards! Yep, we also have rewards listed on the chart, like getting to pick what we have for dinner one night or getting extra screen time. It's really motivating to see what rewards we could earn by completing our chores.

And you know what? We also talk about how proud we feel when we finish a chore, even if starting sometimes felt a bit tough.

So, what about you? What does your Family Chore Chart look like? You can sit with your family and fill out the one on the next page. vv

Name	Chores	M	T	W	Th	F	Sa	Su

Activity 30
Break it Down

"Oops!" I said as I heard the sound of my favorite bowl crashing onto the floor. I really liked that bowl. It was yellow with a picture of a bone on it.

How did I break it, you ask? Well, you see, my parents asked me to help wash the dishes. I wanted to be a helpful member of the family but I was also eager to go and play outside. I rushed through the task and ended up breaking my bowl.

After that accident, my parents sat me down and shared some valuable advice. They explained the importance of taking your time with household tasks and breaking them down into smaller, manageable steps. Together, they helped me make a list of the steps I needed to take to wash the dishes properly.

First, I needed to collect all the dishes from around the house and bring them to the kitchen sink. Then, I had to scrape off any leftover food and rinse the dishes with water. Once that was done, I could put them in the dishwasher and add the detergent. Finally, I had to start the dishwasher and make sure all the dishes were clean and dry before putting them away.

Breaking down the task into smaller steps made it easier and less overwhelming for me to do the dishes.

It also helped me to not rush through them and make sure all the dishes were cleaned properly.

Now, whenever I have a larger household task to do, like cleaning my room or doing the laundry, I break it down into smaller, more achievable steps. It makes it feel less daunting and helps me stay motivated to complete the task.

Here is a list of the most common household tasks. On the right side, break each task into 3 or 4 steps. Here's a super-duper trick to getting started on any task: Think about the very first step you need to take to get started. Usually, the hardest part is simply taking that first step.

Chores:

Set the table for dinner

1. _____
2. _____
3. _____
4. _____

Clean your room

1. _____
2. _____
3. _____
4. _____

Take out the garbage

1. _____
2. _____
3. _____
4. _____

Load the dishwasher

1. _____
2. _____
3. _____
4. _____

....................................(You can add your own chore here)

1. _____
2. _____
3. _____
4. _____

Activity 31
Finding a Home for Everything

It was a lovely Saturday morning. The sun shone brightly in the sky, with puffy white clouds rolling across the horizon. A gentle, warm breeze blew through the open window, with the smell of freshly bloomed flowers and birds chirping in the trees. The air was filled with peaceful energy, making it an ideal day to be outside.

Daisy and I had just finished our breakfast and were ready to head outdoors when Mom and Dad announced that it was time to do some home organization. I must admit, I couldn't help but groan at the thought of cleaning, but my sister Daisy looked thrilled at the prospect of getting our home organized.

Mom explained how decluttering and organizing was important for maintaining a peaceful and orderly living space.

She encouraged us to find designated homes for all our belongings and to label and categorize storage areas.

"A place for everything and everything in its place," Mom said as we got started on our organizing mission.

Mom gave each of us a large basket bag and asked us to start with our own rooms. Initially, I wasn't sure where to start, but Daisy immediately began going through her things and finding homes for them. I followed her lead and did the same. I found crumpled paper, books that were misplaced, and toys that needed to be donated.

After we finished our rooms, we moved on to the living room. Together, we picked up more toys and books and found homes for them. We also labeled storage areas so we could find things easily later on. Labeling was fun. Mom helped us use a label maker but you can also use label stickers. Some of the labels we made were "toys", "legos", and "art supplies".

Now it's your turn: Go around the house with a basket and fill it up with items that are misplaced.

Sort items back into their homes. You can team up with your parents or sibling(s).

Activity 32
The Big Clean-Out

It's that time again, the last weekend of the month, which means it is a big clean-out day for us. Now you know I love having a clean, organized space. It helps me focus and feel at ease. But I have to admit, the thought of doing a big clean was intimidating. It seemed like an overwhelming task that would take all day to complete. However, my mom had a plan that made it seem less daunting. She suggested we break up the tasks into smaller, manageable chunks.

We kicked off our cleaning mission by sorting everything into piles to donate, throw away, or keep.

We decided to tackle one room at a time. We began with the kitchen, taking everything out of the cabinets and tossing anything that had expired. Then, we wiped down the shelves and drawers before putting everything back in an organized manner. Next stop, the living room, where we repeated the process. One by one, we went through each room until the entire house was spotless.

It was a day filled with hard work, but it felt rewarding to see the progress we were making. We blasted music and took breaks when needed to keep our energy up. By the end of the day, our home looked and felt amazing. It was a huge weight off of our shoulders, and we all felt a sense of accomplishment.

As we sat down to relax and enjoy our clean space, I couldn't help but think about how much easier it would be to maintain it. With everything in its place and a designated spot for each item, it would be simple to keep things organized and tidy. Plus, it felt good to know that any items we no longer needed could go to someone in need.

From that day forward, we made a commitment to do a big clean-out every month. It would keep us accountable and prevent clutter from piling up. Plus, it was a fun way to spend quality time as a family while creating a peaceful living environment.

Now it's your turn. Write or draw what your big clean-out looks like.

What room do you want to start with?

What do you enjoy tidying up the most?

Activities and Playtime

Ah, the weekends - what a treat!
Imagine it's a sunny Saturday.

I've got a whole list of fantastic things I want to do. We don't just use our executive functioning skills at home or in school but also on the weekends or in the holidays. We still need to plan our day, start/finish tasks and manage how we feel. In this section, let's talk about skills we can use out in the world.

First on my list for my weekend activities is volunteering at the local animal shelter. I love spending time with animals and lending a helping paw in any way I can. When I arrive, I'm greeted by a group of dogs, eagerly waiting to be walked. I lead them outside and we go for a long stroll in the park. They seem so happy and it makes me feel good, knowing I'm making a difference in their lives.

My day doesn't end there!

Next, I go to the community center to help out with the kids' art class. I'm given the task of setting up an art activity for the kids and getting all the supplies set up. I love seeing their creativity flow and helping them bring their ideas to life. I make sure to listen to each child and encourage them to be proud of their work.

What do you like to do in your community or on the weekend?

Activity 33
Changing Plans.
What Would You Do?

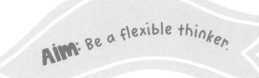
Aim: Be a flexible thinker.

You know, being a smart pup isn't just about reading books and acing school — it's also about being able to be a flexible thinker.

Let me explain. I woke up early on a Saturday morning and I was all hyped up to go to the dog park with my best friend, Max. We had been planning this for weeks, and I couldn't wait to run and play with him all day. But then, my mom came into my room with some not-so-great news. The park was closed due to maintenance. Let me tell you, I was devastated.

I was so set on going to the park that I didn't know what to do. But my mom told me that we could still have a fun day together, just maybe doing something different. She taught me about flexible thinking.

It's the idea that sometimes our plans need to change, but that doesn't mean we can't have fun *in a different way.*

At first, I didn't understand why the park had to be closed. However, my mom explained that maintenance was important to keep the park safe and clean for everyone to enjoy. And then, she asked me what else we could do instead. That's when it clicked — flexible thinking allows us to see a situation from a different angle.

I now understood why the park had to be closed and I also understood my feelings of disappointment. But we decided to go to the beach and had a fantastic day there.

Flexible thinking also allows us to react according to the situation.

For example, I came home today to find that my favorite snack (biscuits and peanut butter) had run out, so I had to choose a different snack to have.

Look at the situations below. Each one requires some flexible thinking. For each situation, write or draw two different ways to think about it:

You're on your way to play baseball with your friends but it's raining, and you have to change your plans.

You have a birthday party to go to that you've been looking forward to, but your friend is feeling ill, and the party has been postponed.

You're on your way to have dinner with your family at your favorite restaurant, but it's closed for renovation.

You want to play a board game with your friends, but they all want to play hide-and-go-seek.

Activity 34
Think Before Speaking

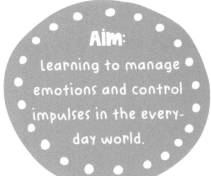

I was playing catch with my friend, Jake, in the park. We were having a great time tossing the ball back and forth, but then Jake accidentally threw the ball too hard, and it hit me in the face. My instant reaction was to say something mean to Jake, even though I didn't really mean it. I told him he was a baby and didn't know how to throw.

Jake looked hurt and upset, and I immediately regretted my words. I realized that I said something unkind without thinking and felt bad about it. I apologized to Jake and explained that I didn't mean to say what I said.

Jake forgave me, and we continued to play catch. But I couldn't shake off the feeling that I should have thought before speaking. I knew that saying hurtful things could hurt others, even if I didn't mean to hurt Jake.

After that, I decided to try and think before speaking.

Whenever I felt a strong emotion, I would take a deep breath and try to calm down. I would think about what I wanted to say and how it might make the other person feel. If it was a negative comment, I would try to rephrase it in a more positive way.

Now, I still get excited and angry sometimes, but I'm learning how to manage those emotions better. I think before speaking, and I try to choose my words wisely. It's not always easy, but it's worth it.

Here's a super handy tool to help you decide if it's a good idea to say what we are thinking. It's called THINK:

T Is it True? Yes No

H Is it Helpful? Yes No

I Is it Important? Yes No

N Is it Necessary? Yes No

K Is it Kind? Yes No

If you answered yes to all five questions, then it's a good idea to say what you're thinking.

Activity 35
The Memory Game

Do you ever forget things? I certainly do! I used to forget where I left my toys, what my friend had told me earlier, or what I had to do after school. But I've been working on my memory skills. You see, memory helps us in all sorts of situations. It helps us remember what our friends or teacher just said, what we need to do that day, and even while having a conversation. It is a brain superpower that we can work on.

My friend, the wise old owl, noticed how forgetful I could get and taught me a few memory games. I'll share these with you:

1. Memory Match: Turn over cards with pictures or words on them and try to match pairs. Start with a small number of cards and gradually increase the difficulty as your memory improves.

2. I Spy: Look around your room or outside and choose an object to spy on. After a few seconds, close your eyes and try to remember as many details about the object as possible.

3. Repeat After Me: Have a friend or your parent say a series of words or numbers, and then try to repeat them back in the same order.

4. Simon Says: Play the classic game of following commands given by "Simon" but add a twist by requiring players to remember the sequence of commands given.

5. Storytelling: Take turns telling a story, adding one sentence at a time. Each player must remember the previous sentences in order to continue the story.

By playing fun memory games like these, you can strengthen your working memory and improve your ability to remember important information.

Activity 36
Setting Goals

I've always been a creature of habit. I find comfort in my cozy routines, like napping on my favorite cushion or chasing after my beloved frisbee. Yet I have also come to recognize the importance of setting goals so I can achieve them.

I learned about setting goals from my mom and dad. They set goals too! Yesterday I was having a chat with my parents about what my goals were for the year. They asked me to write down what my goals were. My mom told me that a goal is something we want to achieve and that we need to have a plan to make it happen.

> You see, goals are like the destination on a map,
> and the plan is the route we take to get there.

I thought about it for a while, and I decided that my goal for the year was to read 15 books. I love to read, but I always find myself getting distracted by other things and not reading as much as I want to. I have other goals too. I want to take up a new sport and win the school art contest this year.

I made a plan for each goal. You see, goals without plans are hard to achieve (remember the plan is how you're going to get there). So, for example, for my reading goal, I set aside 20 minutes each day to read, and keep track of how many books I read.

Remember that having a goal means sticking to your plan even if you feel frustrated or discouraged. You got this!

Oh, and don't forget to reward yourself when you reach your goals.

Fill out the page below with your goals, action plan, and the reward.

Goal 1:

- -

Action Plan:

- -

- -

Reward:

- -

Goal 2:

- -

Action Plan:

- -

- -

Reward:

- -

Activity 37
Calm Breathing

Aim:
Learn breathing techniques to manage stress and regulate emotions.

Guess what? I found out that I have to act in the school play. Now, normally, I'm not one to shy away from attention but this time it's different. I was feeling overwhelmed and stressed out. What if I forgot my lines? What if I messed up my cues? What if everyone made fun of me?

My heart was racing, and my mind was racing even faster. I knew that I needed to do something to calm down and get centered.

I remembered what I had learned about calm breathing. So, I decided to give it a shot.

I closed my eyes and took a deep breath in through my nose. I held it for a few seconds and then slowly breathed out through my mouth. It felt weird at first, but as I continued to breathe like this, I felt my body start to relax.

I started to think about the positives. I loved being on stage and performing for people. I've always been confident, and I knew that I had the ability to do this. Plus, my friends and family were going to be there to support me.

I took a deep breath and focused on my belly rising and falling with each breath in and breath out. I felt my body start to relax as I continued to breathe slowly and deeply.

Here are some breathing techniques for you to try: (PS. My favorite one is the belly breathing!)

Belly breathing: Lie down on your back and place one hand on your chest and the other on your belly. Take deep breaths in through the nose, feeling your belly expand, nd then breathe out slowly through your mouth, feeling your belly go back down. Focus your attention on your breathing and the movement of your belly. How did that feel?

Counted breathing: Sit or lie down comfortably and breathe in slowly through your nose for a count of four. Then hold your breath for a count of four and breathe out slowly through your mouth for a count of four. Repeat this cycle for several minutes.

Square breathing: Imagine drawing a square in your mind. As you breathe in, imagine tracing one side of the square, holding your breath as you trace another side, breathing out as you trace a third side, and holding your breath once again as you trace the last side.

Practice these techniques during stressful situations or before important tasks.

conclusion

Congratulations young explorer! What an incredible journey you've been on with Ronny. You've discovered how to become the CEO of your brain and learned a lot of cool new skills. With these tricks in your pocket, you're unstoppable!

Executive functioning skills are important brain superpowers that allow us to plan, prioritize, focus, and manage time.

In this workbook, we covered important skills such as goal-setting, time management, organizing, planning, and self-regulation. These skills are crucial for academic success, personal growth, and achievement in various areas of life.

As you continue to practice and develop these skills, it will become easier to achieve your goals and overcome challenges.

Remember to use strategies such as planning, breaking tasks into smaller steps, and self-evaluation to improve your performance.

By investing in your executive functioning skills, you are setting yourself up for success in school and beyond. Keep up the good work and keep learning and growing!

You got this!

Exercise Index

About the Author:

Bibi S Shah, PhD, is a Child Therapist and Developmental Psychologist with nearly two decades of experience in the field of child development. Bibi has devoted her career to helping children and parents navigate the complex terrain of emotional well-being and growth.

In this book, Bibi shares her insights and wisdom with a broader audience, translating her years of practical experience into accessible resources for parents and caregivers. Her writing reflects a deep understanding of the challenges children face in today's world and provides practical strategies to empower them to maximize their potential.

Made in the USA
Coppell, TX
03 April 2024

30861412R00052